D1048096

BRINGING IT HOME

A Post-Trip Devotional Guide for International and Domestic Short-Term Mission Teams

JIM MERSEREAU

Foresight

ForesightPublishingNow.com

Copyright 2010 by Jim Mersereau
(Copyright applied for)

Bringing It Home
by: Jim Mersereau

The Bible translation used was the New International Version
copyright 1984 by the International Bible Society.

Printed in the United States of America

ISBN 9780984442348

All rights reserved solely by the author. The author guaran-
tees all contents are original and do not infringe upon the legal
rights of any other person or work. No part of this book may
reproduced in any form without the permission of the author.
The views expressed in this book are not necessarily those of
the publisher.

FORESIGHT BOOK PUBLISHING
ForesightPublishingNow.com

Dedication

To my wife Linda.

The Lord called me to be a sailor, pastor, and mission team leader and He gave me the perfect wife for such a life. During all those years in the Navy, while I was off sailing around the world, you were the anchor and the stabilizing influence in our family. For many more years after that you have waited patiently while I was off in Mexico, Peru, Romania, or wherever the latest mission trip took me. For over thirty-two years, with love, good humor, and a positive attitude, you have managed things on the home front, cared for and nurtured our children, and encouraged me in my calling. I could not have asked for a better life partner – a true soul mate.

Our life together has been rich, full, rewarding and fun. One thing it has not been is dull! I love your sweet gentle spirit and your endless capacity for grace. I love your firm resolve and your refusal to give up when things get tough. I love your smile and your laugh. I love your lasagna. Thanks for believing in me.

TABLE OF CONTENTS

SUGGESTIONS FOR TEAM LEADERS:

Helping your team members get the most from this devotional guide

Mission trips change lives. You already know that to be true. So often the mission turns out to have been more about what God wanted to do *in* a person rather than *through* them. Short-term missions can be defining, even transforming events in a person's life. But the opportunity to learn and grow from this experience shouldn't stop the day the mission ends. Often the greatest, most revealing lessons are learned in retrospect – in the days and weeks after returning home. That's the purpose of, *"Bringing It Home – A post-trip devotional guide for short-term mission teams."*

This devotional guide is a tool designed to lead short-termers to prayerfully think through their mission experience, gain insight into what God was teaching them, and learn how those lessons should make a difference in the practice of their faith at home.

As the Team Leader you can help team members achieve this. Here are a few tips to help you guide your team members to get the most from this devotional guide:

▶ Hold a group meeting the last day on the mission field. At that time present each team member with a copy of "Bringing It Home". Review the guide with them, emphasizing the importance of the "post-trip" period. Explain that some of the most valuable insights and lessons learned will come as they prayerfully consider their experience in retrospect.

▶ During the group meeting direct team member's attention to the day 13 devotion "The Big Presentation." If team members are scheduled to give a group presentation prior to completing the day 13 devotion, they will want to skip ahead and complete that day's lesson prior to their presentation.

▶ If most of your team members are from the same location (such as a church group), plan to have a group meeting two weeks after returning home. Make it a fun occasion with food and fellowship. This will be a great opportunity for team members to share memories of the mission and tell stories about their favorite experiences.

▶ During the meeting be sure to allow time for the group to discuss what they learned from "Bringing It Home." This will be an opportunity for you as the Team Leader to help individual team members further process the learning experience and for the group to learn from each other.

▶ If most of your team members are not from the same location you can still help them through the post-trip period. During the group meeting on the last day on the mission field, encourage team members to commit to share their post-trip insights with the rest of the group via email. As the team leader you can help facilitate the exchange of learning experiences during the post-trip period by sending periodic group emails prompting team members to share what they've learned.

▶ Reestablish contact with all team members six months after returning home. Ask them to report on the changes God has brought about in their lives as a result of their mission experience. Such testimonies can be inspiring if shared with the rest of the team, and they can also serve as great recruiting tools for future mission teams.

FORWARD

by Bud and Jane Fray

To any serious follower of Jesus who has gone "on mission with God", this guide is a must. The highest calling on earth to believers is to be "laborers together with God." What a glorious concept and privilege!

Having gone on your recent mission project, you dare not lose anything the Holy Spirit has said or taught you. This devotional guide will be invaluable as a study help or evaluation tool to maximize your Lord's investment in you. And what an investment it was, right?

This guide will increase your usefulness and availability for your next assignment as well as your present responsibility. Who knows, the next project may be sooner than you think. After all, the loving heart of our great God and heavenly Father is brooding powerfully over our planet. We must be committed and ready.

Dear Jesus-follower, please allow your Lord to use this guide to assist you in processing what you have seen and done. The experience must be preserved in your life and used in your present service in your local Church. But most of all, you have grown in your experience and knowledge of the Lord. Don't lose that.

Do you see it? The processing at the end is just as valuable as your preparation at the beginning of the project. It could, by the grace of God, be even more valuable. Our God of all blessing is able to make all grace abound toward you, and make you fruitful to every good work. Your next assignment can be the most productive you have ever been on. Be excited about being ready!

One other thought comes to mind at this point. We do not know the day or the hour when our Lord shall return. We have a growing and even urgent sense that *you* could be a part of the ultimate group of Kingdom harvesters. So dig in with all your heart. Enjoy your journey through this guide. Your "well done thy good and faithful servant" could depend on how you tackle this part of your past trip and your preparation for the next.

"How beautiful are the feet of those who bring glad tidings of good things." (Romans 10:15).

Keep your feet and your heart ready until *all* have heard the Good News.

Your fellow servants in His service,
Bud and Jane Fray
Retired Southern Baptist Missionaries
Zimbabwe, Africa

INTRODUCTION

Short-term missions change lives. That's a truth we see validated on trip after trip. On the mission field short-termers participate in the work of God in ways they never have before.

Removed from the routine of everyday life, our normal problems and concerns are often just distant memories. With our daily attention fully focused on the work of the mission, team members commonly experience a heightened sense of spiritual awareness. Sometimes we can hear the voice of God more clearly while on a distant mission field than we ever can at home. Therefore the mission often turns out to have been more about what God wanted to do *in* you than *through* you.

It's not unusual for short-termers to speak of the mission trip as having been a "mountaintop experience". Salvations, rededicated lives, new insights into God's leading for career choices, a call to ministry, and new friendships are all common occurrences.

Yes, short-term missions can be special, life-changing events – true "mountaintop" experiences. But what do you do with it once the mission is over? How do you process those experiences and hang onto them? How do you bring it all home with you? That's the purpose of this devotional guide.

"Bringing It Home" includes fourteen daily devotions designed to help you prayerfully think through your short-term mission experience, and to grow from it in such a way that you become a stronger, more dynamic Christian. You will find the "Journaling" pages at the end of each day's devotion to be especially helpful. When God speaks we should always write it down. So be sure to record the insights He reveals to you regarding your short-term mission.

Here at CERT International we like to tell pastors that if they will send their people on short-term missions with us, we'll send them back as better church members. It's our prayer that will be true of you too.

DAY ONE

A Job Well Done

*At the end of a busy mission trip an exhausted
nurse waits for her flight home.*

So, how was your short-term mission trip? Was it exciting? Rewarding? How about fulfilling, challenging, heart-touching, and life-changing? It was probably all of that and much more.

In all likelihood right now you're basking in the warm afterglow of a job well done – and you should be! You stepped out in faith, offered yourself to the Lord to be used in a very special way, made big sacrifices in terms of time and financial commitments, traveled far to minister to people in great need, and you did it all for the glory of God.

Now you're probably physically tired and emotionally drained–but in a good way. Short-term missions can be exhausting. So the first day home is usually a day of rest and reflection as you prepare to reenter your world of school, jobs, family and friends.

Take some time now to read 2 Timothy 4:7-8:

As the Apostle Paul reflected on his own ministry do you think he felt he had been faithful and tried to do his best for the Lord? What did he write that makes you think so?

Does it seem as if Paul believed the Lord was pleased with his service? Again, cite your reasons.

When he wrote 2 Timothy, Paul was nearing the end of his life and was reflecting on a lifetime of ministry. I'm only asking you to reflect on the brief period of your short-term mission but still, the example applies.

As you recall your short-term mission you'll probably remember some things you wish you had done better. But if you're fair in your evaluation you'll also realize there were many things you did well. Cite some examples of how you did your best to serve the Lord on this mission:

_____

_____

_____

_____

_____

Do you believe the Lord was pleased with your service? Why or why not?

_____

_____

_____

_____

Read Matthew 25:31-40

Think about the people you served on your mission trip. Remember the faces and the expressions of gratitude. What people and events stand out in your mind as being particularly special?

_____

_____

_____

_____

Day One Journaling

Spend some quiet time with God. Let the sense of your Heavenly Father's pleasure wash over and envelope you. Hear Him say to you, "Well done, my good and faithful servant." When you are done, take some time to record your thoughts.

_____

_____

_____

_____

_____

_____

_____

_____

_____

_____

_____

_____

_____

_____

_____

_____

_____

_____

_____

DAY TWO

Mountains and Valleys

A mountaintop experience in the Andes Mountains of Peru.

As you continue the reentry process you're probably becoming aware of the stark differences between what you experienced on the mission field and your normal everyday life.

The mission field was exciting, challenging, and spiritually exhilarating. Life at home is, well ..., its life at home. Compared to the project you were just involved in, your normal life could seem a little dull and maybe even boring. So let's talk for a moment about mountaintops and valleys.

As has already been noted in this guide, short-term missions are often compared to "mountaintop experiences". That's because mountaintops are special places. Mountaintops are usually not where you live. They're hard to get to and once you're there, it's often a spectacular experience.

Valleys on the other hand *are* where most people live. They're easy to get to and usually aren't all that special. Most of life is lived in the valleys not on the mountaintops.

Do you see the analogy? Short-term missions are special, sometimes even spectacular experiences. But most of life is not. Most of life is routine, repetitive and unremarkable. Yet it's the very normalcy of everyday life that makes something like a short-term mission so special.

Sometimes short-termers are bothered by the obvious disconnect between the special experience of a mission trip and life at home. Many times they even find they're now dissatisfied with their regular life and want it to be more like what they experienced on the mission field. Well, that's *exactly* what God intended!

Read Philippians 1:4-6

Remember I said that short-term mission trips change lives? On the mission field God allowed you to experience some special things – things that have touched your heart and changed you. In those moments God began a new work in you that He intends to continue. Take time now to remember some of those special moments and experiences. Write them here:

_____

_____

_____

_____

_____

What do you think God was trying to show you, or teach you, through those special times on the mission field?

_____

_____

_____

_____

_____

_____

_____

What changes in your normal life (life in the valley), do you think God wants you to make as a result of what you experienced on the mountain-top of your short-term mission?

Are there some ministry activities you could be involved in here at home that would be similar to what you were involved in on the mission trip?

_____

_____

_____

_____

_____

_____

_____

Day Two Journaling

How should your life at home be different as a result of your short-term mission experience? Take some time to sit quietly before the Lord and let Him speak to you about all this. When you're done, record your thoughts.

_____

_____

_____

_____

_____

_____

_____

_____

_____

_____

_____

_____

_____

_____

_____

_____

_____

_____

_____

DAY THREE

The Big Letdown

A Physician's Assistant makes new friends on the mission field. Leaving them when its time to go home can be a sad thing.

As you ease back into your normal routine it's not unusual to experience feelings of regret that the trip is over, or maybe some sadness as you realize you miss the new friends you made, or sometimes even a bit of low-grade depression. It's important to realize those emotions are normal and commonly experienced after a successful short-term mission.

Let's take some time right now to read about when the Old Testament prophet Elijah went through something similar. Begin by reading 1 Kings 18:16-40:

Do you think it required a great step of faith on Elijah's part to confront King Ahab and then take-on the prophets of Baal like he did? Where do you think Elijah got the courage to do that?

_____

_____

_____

On your short-term mission were there times when you had to simply step out in faith, trusting the Lord to work things out? Describe one of those times:

_____

_____

_____

From that experience what did you learn about God and about yourself?

_____

_____

_____

_____

Now read 1 Kings 19:1-4:

What happened to Elijah? How did he go so quickly from being a powerful, victorious prophet of God in chapter 18, to the frightened, cowering man we read about in these verses?

_____

_____

_____

_____

As I noted earlier, short-term missions can be physically and emotionally exhausting. They can also be spiritually draining. There's often a lot of intense spiritual warfare taking place during the mission and like Elijah we can end up spiritually spent.

Since your return home have you sensed that you might be suffering from a bit of spiritual exhaustion?

_____

_____

_____

Now read 1 Kings 19:5-8:

What did the angel of the Lord do to help Elijah recharge his spiritual batteries?

_____

_____

_____

Often what we need most after an intense period of ministry is some simple rest and relaxation. Like Elijah in 1 Kings 19, sometimes the most spiritual thing we can do is take a nap!

Day Three Journaling

Spend some time sitting quietly before the Lord. Ask Him to help you accurately assess your current spiritual condition. Then ask Him what He wants you to do so He can renew and refresh you. Perhaps an extended time of prayer, or maybe some time reading the Psalms or, He may just want you to take a nap! When you're done, record what He said to you.

_____

_____

_____

_____

_____

_____

_____

_____

_____

_____

_____

_____

_____

_____

_____

_____

_____

_____

_____

DAY FOUR

Life in a Different Dimension

A dental clinic in a remote village in Peru.
Conditions on the mission field are often very different
from what we are used to at home.

So you've been home for a few days now. As you've resumed your normal activities at school, work, home and church you've probably been speaking to people about your mission trip. Have you noticed a difference between the degree of your enthusiasm and their level of interest? Does it seem like you're a lot more fired-up about it than they are?

Sometimes short-termers report being disappointed and frustrated that people at home don't seem to be as excited or interested in the results of the short-term mission as they are.

During such times it's important to remember that you've had a very special experience on your mission trip–an experience your friends and family haven't had. While you were exploring spiritual mountaintops, engaging in unique forms of ministry, and enjoying special fellowship with the Lord, they were back home slugging it out in their daily routines.

So now, as you enthusiastically share your experiences with them, it can sometimes seem as if they're just not getting it–as if you're each living in different dimensions and you can see things they can't. That can be frustrating.

When that happens it's important to check your attitude.

Read Philippians 2:3-11:

What do you think Paul's main point in this passage was?

_____

_____

_____

In verse 5 Paul says our attitude should be the same as that of Christ Jesus. What one word would you choose to describe the attitude Paul was referring to?

_____

_____

_____

_____

The word you probably chose was "humble" or "humility". How does that lesson apply to this process of reentering life after a short-term mission trip? What would your "post-mission trip attitude" look like if it was characterized by the humility of Jesus?

_____

_____

_____

Often our experiences on the mission field were so special that we return home with a strong desire for our family and friends to feel what we felt and to see things from the same new perspective we have gained. If they don't, it can sometimes result in disappointment and frustration. And if we aren't careful, that can easily morph into a "holier-than-thou" attitude. We must guard against that. Here are a few tips you may find helpful:

▶ Pray about the post-trip period as much as you did for the pre-trip.

▶ Try to wait until your family and friends ask you to speak about your mission experience. When they do, they will be demonstrating their interest in your trip and will pay much closer attention to what you share.

▶ Be sure to emphasize what *God* did rather than what you did. Talk about how He used you to accomplish His purposes. Give Him the credit and glory.

_____

_____

_____

_____

_____

_____

_____

_____

Day Four Journaling

Spend some quiet time with the Lord. Ask Him to show you any adjustments you may need to make to your attitude. Ask him to help you understand how you can share your experiences with others in a way that is enthusiastic but at the same time kind, humble and understanding. When you are done, record your thoughts.

_____

_____

_____

_____

_____

_____

_____

_____

_____

_____

_____

_____

_____

_____

_____

_____

_____

DAY FIVE

What Difference did it make over There?

Mission teams are often successfull at leading people
to faith in Jesus. They can also help to strengthen the local
churches they work in support of on the mission field.

By now you've probably told lots of stories and shown all the pictures from your short-term mission, maybe many times already. And surely there's a lot to tell – people you met, things you saw, projects completed, spiritual victories.

As you've relived those memories have you found yourself wondering if your team really made any *lasting* difference while you were there? If so then join the crowd. At some point most of us have brief moments of doubt like that.

Since short-term missions are by definition "short", they are also limited in what they can accomplish. But that doesn't mean the mission wasn't meaningful or that it didn't make a difference. Let's consider three ways in which your short-term mission may have made a meaningful difference over there:

First, reread Matthew 25:31-40.

How important is it to Jesus for His followers to engage in intentional acts of compassion that help relieve the physical suffering of people?

_____

_____

_____

_____

_____

_____

On your short-term mission did your team participate in acts of compassion to relieve physical suffering in any way? (This could include medical and dental clinics, constructing or renovating buildings, preparing meals, playing with orphans, etc ...) List some of them here:

_____

_____

_____

_____

_____

_____

_____

Physical ministry and acts of compassion–no matter how limited, do make a difference.

Next, read Isaiah 52:7.

How does God feel about those who are willing to travel far to share the Good News of salvation through Jesus?

_____

_____

_____

_____

_____

On your short-term mission did your team participate in evangelistic activities? What were they and what results are you aware of? (Note: Sometimes the results of our evangelistic efforts won't be fully revealed until we're in heaven.)

_____

_____

_____

_____

Finally, read Exodus 17:8-13.

Who would you say was the *primary* minister in this scene?

_____

_____

_____

_____

What role did Aaron and Hur play?

_____

_____

_____

_____

Was it an important role? Do you think Moses would have been as successful in his ministry without their assistance?

_____

_____

_____

_____

On your short-term mission, who were the local Christians your team worked in support of? (Perhaps they were American missionaries, or local pastors and their churches.) Write some of their names here:

_____

_____

_____

_____

_____

Do you think the efforts of your team helped to encourage those local Christians? Do you think you helped to strengthen their ministries? In what ways?

_____

_____

_____

_____

_____

Now let's return to our original question: "What difference did it make over there?" Think in terms of physical ministry, evangelism and encouraging the local Christians in their ministries.

_____

_____

_____

_____

_____

_____

_____

_____

_____

_____

_____

_____

_____

Day Five Journaling

It is a privilege to be used by God to help in His Kingdom-building work. As you think about the ways He used you and your team, the things that were accomplished, remember to give Him the credit and thank Him for allowing you to be a part of it. Spend some quiet time with the Lord now. When you are done, record your thoughts here:

_____

_____

_____

_____

_____

_____

_____

_____

_____

_____

_____

_____

_____

_____

_____

_____

_____

_____

DAY SIX

What Difference did it make over Here?

Romanian woman in a remote village in the Transylvania region. The joy of knowing Jesus can be seen on her face.

Hopefully after your time with the Lord yesterday, you now have no doubts about the value of what your team accomplished over there, but how about over here?

When a short-term mission team goes from one place to serve in another, does the mission have any positive impact on the sending church?

Read Luke 6:38:

In this verse Jesus was illustrating the Biblical principle of sowing and reaping, which is also taught in many other passages.

The principle holds that whatever we sow God will ensure we reap in like manner. So if we sow trouble we will reap it in return (Job 4:8); if we give generously to those in need, God will see to it we are blessed in return (Proverbs 22:9, 2 Corinthians 9:6); if we have regard for the weak and needy, God will look out for us as well (Psalm 41:1-3).

In Luke 6:38 Jesus was making reference to a general Biblical principle which teaches that whenever we go out of our way to be a blessing to others, God has His ways of returning that blessing to us many times over.

That brings us back to the subject of your short-term mission. We've already established in our Day One devotion that God is pleased with your ministry efforts on this mission. Then on Day Two you thought about some of the changes God is bringing about in your own life through the experiences of your trip. So now let's talk about how all of that impacts your local church here at home.

I remember an example from a mission to the Central Romanian province of Transylvania. The team was holding medical and dental clinics in a little farming village. While the clinics were going on, an American pastor and three of his church members, along with a translator, were walking the dirt streets of the village – just praying and inviting people to the clinic.

At one point they came across an old woman harvesting potatoes in a field. They tried to engage her in conversation but the woman politely told them she had too much work to do so she couldn't stop to talk.

The three American church members then offered to harvest the potatoes for her so she could take some time to speak with the pastor. A big smile spread across the woman's face as she readily agreed.

During the conversation the pastor answered many spiritual questions for her and explained the plan of salvation–which resulted in the woman placing her faith in Jesus for the forgiveness of her sins. And, she ended up with three times as many potatoes harvested than if she had done the work herself! The woman was saved, the potatoes were harvested, but it was actually the three American church members who received the much bigger blessing.

That night at dinner, as they related the story to their fellow team members, they were absolutely glowing! You see, by going out of their way to be a blessing to someone else in the Name of Jesus, the Lord blessed their hearts. They had a mission experience they will never forget!

Although you already did this on Day One, spend some additional time now thinking about the special things you experienced on your mission trip. Write some of them here:

_____

_____

_____

_____

_____

_____

_____

_____

_____

_____

_____

_____

_____

_____

_____

Now go back to the Day Two devotion and think a little more about the changes the Lord is bringing about in your life as a result of your mission experience. Write some of them here:

_____

_____

_____

_____

_____

_____

_____

_____

_____

_____

_____

_____

Remember in the introduction to this devotional guide I made the statements that mission trips change lives and that people return to their home churches as better church members? Do you think those statements are true?

_____

Are they true of you?

_____

Will you be a better church member as a result of the things you experienced on your short-term mission? If so, in what ways?

_____

_____

_____

_____

_____

_____

_____

So, did your short-term mission make a difference over here too?

_____

_____

_____

_____

_____

_____

_____

Day Six Journaling

As you now sit quietly before the Lord, allow the Holy Spirit to bring to your mind images of the kind of church member you were before your mission trip. Then invite Him to give you a vision of what your future involvement in the fellowship should look like. Spend some quiet time with the Lord then record your thoughts here.

_____

_____

_____

_____

_____

_____

_____

_____

_____

_____

_____

_____

_____

_____

_____

_____

_____

_____

DAY SEVEN

A Larger Vision

A worship service in a village in the Philippines.
True worship is from the heart and knows no boundaries
of culture, generation or tradition.

Our short-term mission team was participating in Sunday morning worship in a small church in the Transylvania region of Romania.

On our team were Christians from four different regions of the United States, plus a pastor from Mexico and a Malaysian medical doctor who lived in Great Britain. Seven different denominational backgrounds were represented by our team members. In the Romanian congregation we were worshipping with there were Romanians, Hungarians, and ethnic Gypsies.

The setting was formal – men in coats and ties, women in dresses and head scarves; men sat on the left side of the church, women on the right. The service was highly structured but the singing was angelic, the prayers were passionate and many of the worshipers openly wept throughout the service.

Come with me now to another worship service with a different mission team – this time in a small jungle village in the Southern Amazon Basin of Peru. It was Sunday night and the local believers were meeting in the community pavilion in the center of the village. The building consisted of nothing more than a wooden floor, thatch roof and no walls. The night sounds of the jungle were loud all around us.

This setting was very informal. Most of the people wore dirty, tattered clothing and were barefoot. They sat cross-legged on the floor. The service was loose and unstructured as people sang, gave testimonies and prayed as led by the Spirit. The pastor gave a short sermon and an invitation. And just as in the Romanian service, many worshippers were visibly moved– responding with tears, confessions, and renewed commitments.

Read Revelation 7:9-10:

In this passage the Apostle John tells of a heavenly worship service that included people from every nation, tribe, people group and language. A multi-cultural gathering if there ever was one!

On your short-term mission did you participate in cross-cultural worship services?

What were they like? Did you sense the presence of God in the service even if you couldn't understand the language being used?

Did you gain a new understanding of the truth that genuine worship is a matter of the heart that transcends language and culture?

_____

_____

_____

Has your cross-cultural missions experience expanded your understanding of the work of God worldwide? If so, in what ways?

_____

_____

_____

_____

For almost 2000 years the Holy Spirit has been crossing cultural, generational, and language barriers to impact people in ways that are meaningful in their life settings. Did your cross-cultural missions experience help you appreciate this truth in a new, fresh way?

_____

_____

_____

_____

How will this new understanding impact the practice of your faith now that you're home?

_____

_____

_____

_____

Day Seven Journaling

It has been rightly said that *every* human heart yearns for God. That's true even if the individual doesn't realize it is God they are seeking. Every human being has a place in their heart that can only be filled by God. Therefore the worship of God is in no way limited by generation, custom, culture, tradition or personal preference. How does that truth change your understanding of worship? Spend some quiet time with the Lord now. Record your thoughts when you're done.

_____

_____

_____

_____

_____

_____

_____

_____

_____

_____

_____

_____

_____

_____

_____

_____

_____

DAY EIGHT

Working Together, Serving Others

A successful mission requires team work.

Bill Knepper, of DELTA Ministries International, tells the following story in his contribution to "The Next Mile": [1]

"The story is told of a man who was given a tour of hell. The tables were piled high with delicious food; roast turkey, mashed potatoes, fruit salads, and every kind of pie. However, he was shocked to see that all those sitting at the tables were thin and starving. He noticed they all had to use four-foot long forks taped to their hands! They could see the food. They could even load the fork, but because it was so long, they could never get it to their mouths. They suffered in agony.

Then he was taken to heaven. Surprised, he saw the same thing! Tables loaded with food and forks four feet long taped to each person's hand. However, everyone was plump and happy. The difference was in what they did with the forks. Those in heaven fed each other." (Used by permission)

Read John 13:1-17:

What lesson was Jesus teaching His disciples?

_____

_____

_____

_____

_____

_____

Why do you think Peter objected to Jesus washing his feet?

_____

_____

_____

_____

_____

In your own experience, is it easier for you to serve someone else or to allow them to serve you? Why?

_____

_____

_____

_____

_____

_____

On your short-term mission were there times when you served other team members? Describe one of those times:

_____

_____

_____

_____

_____

_____

_____

How did it make you feel to provide that service to others?

_____

_____

_____

_____

_____

_____

Were there times when other team members served you? Describe one
of those times:

_____

_____

_____

_____

_____

_____

_____

_____

How did it make you feel to be on the receiving end of that act of service?

_____

_____

_____

_____

_____

It has been said: "There is the grace of giving, but there is also the grace of receiving". What do you think that means?

_____

_____

_____

_____

How important was it for team members to serve each other and work together on your mission trip?

_____

_____

_____

How important is it for church members to do the same here at home?

_____

_____

_____

Now that you've had this experience of serving and of being served on your mission trip, what difference will it make in your life here at home?

_____

_____

_____

_____

Sources:

1. Bill Knepper - Contributing Author; "The Next Mile: Short-Term Missions for the Long Haul". 2005, Authentic Media, 1932805613

Day Eight Journaling

Partnership, unity, sharing one another's burdens, just as those were crucial elements of a successful mission trip, they are also essential to healthy church life. Spend some quiet time with the Lord and allow Him to speak to you about this. When you're done, record your thoughts.

_____

_____

_____

_____

_____

_____

_____

_____

_____

_____

_____

_____

_____

_____

_____

_____

_____

DAY NINE

Jesus Makes the Difference

Life is hard for many people we
meet on the mission field.

So what did you think of the living conditions you witnessed while you were on your short-term mission? Did you see people living in conditions far worse than what you are used to at home?

Short-term mission teams from affluent nations typically go to places that are very poor by comparison. Extreme poverty, poor sanitation, lack of adequate healthcare and advanced malnutrition are all situations short-termers commonly encounter.

As you were being exposed to those situations did it occur to you that in only a short time you would be home, enjoying a relatively comfortable standard of living, while the people in the place you visited would remain there in those same conditions?

While you were thinking about that you may also have realized that all physical ministry is temporary at best. No matter how good the care they receive in the medical clinic, someday that person will get sick again and someday they will die. The building you constructed will eventually deteriorate and fall down. The well you dug will only produce fresh water for a limited number of years. The meals you prepared nourished the people for that day, but the next day they were hungry again.

As important and meaningful as the physical ministry was, if you are like most of us then at some point you found yourself yearning to give them more–something permanent rather than temporary. You may have wondered, "Isn't there something short-term mission teams can leave behind that will make a difference in the lives of the people long after the team is gone?"

The answer of course, is "yes". We can give them Jesus. Jesus can transform even the most dreary and difficult life into one of great joy.

Read Matthew 11:28-30:

Does the imagery Jesus used in this passage describe the people you ministered to on your mission trip? Were they weary, burdened, in need of rest?

In this passage Jesus painted a word picture the people of His day could easily relate to. Being a farming society, they were used to seeing teams of oxen yoked together working in the fields. The people knew that in every team of oxen there was a lead ox and a follower ox. The lead ox was bigger, stronger and more experienced. Therefore the lead ox carries most of the load and provides the direction. The follower ox walks alongside the lead ox, sharing the burden and joining in the work, all the while learning from the lead ox.

In this lesson Jesus was saying "Let me be your lead ox." "Come alongside me and we will walk through this life together. I will carry most of the load and I will provide the direction. Just stick close to me and we will do this together."

What will happen if a person will choose to walk through life yoked to Jesus? Verse 29 tells us: "You will find rest for your souls." Why is that true? Verse 30 says: "For my yoke is easy and my burden is light."

You see, life is so much easier with Jesus than without Him. Regardless of the circumstances, Jesus can transform any life into one of great joy and victory. Whether that life is lived in a grass hut in Africa, or in a mansion in Beverly Hills, or in your home town, Jesus wants to walk through it with us.

Of course the true benefit of knowing Jesus as Lord and Savior is the gift of eternal salvation. That's the prize that awaits every believer. But in addition to that, *this life* will always be so much better with Him than without Him.

In what ways did your mission team introduce people to Jesus?

_____

_____

_____

_____

_____

Can you see what a difference that will make in their lives now, in addition to the obvious benefit of eternal salvation?

_____

_____

_____

Just as the people you met on your mission trip needed Jesus, so too do the people you meet every day here at home. What are some ways you could be more intentional about introducing your family, friends and neighbors to Jesus?

_____

_____

_____

_____

_____

Finally, do you know Jesus as your personal Lord and Savior? If not, why not invite Him into your life right now?

Day Nine Journaling

Slowly reread Matthew 11:28-30 then spend some quiet time with the Lord. Thank Him for the privilege of being able to go on this mission trip to help hurting people and to tell them about Jesus. When you are done, record your thoughts.

_____

_____

_____

_____

_____

_____

_____

_____

_____

_____

_____

_____

_____

_____

_____

_____

_____

_____

DAY TEN

Share the Blessings

Many people in our world today still live in extreme poverty.

Chances are your short-term mission was to a country or region that is much more impoverished than where you live. Most people who live in one of the highly developed nations of the world enjoy a standard of living unknown to the majority of people on this planet. Large parts of the rest of the world are extremely poor by comparison.

▶ 1.4 billion people live on less than $1.25 per day. [1]

▶ Another 4.7 billion live in low or middle-low income economies. [2]

▶ 820 million people in the world are undernourished. [3]

▶ Every day almost 16,000 children die from hunger related causes – almost one child every five seconds. [4]

▶ 80% of all diseases in developing nations are caused by contaminated drinking water, claiming the lives of more than five million children per year. [5]

▶ The wealthiest nations make-up less than 20% of the world's population but consume more than 80% of the world's resources – leaving less than 20% of the resources for more than 80% of the population. [6]

Statistics like that can easily leave us feeling depressed and maybe even a little guilty, but that's not necessary. God, in His divine wisdom, has chosen to allow your country to have the level of abundance you have. And He has chosen to allow you to live in that country, at this time in history, rather than anywhere else at any other time. So we don't have to feel guilty about what we have, but we do need to recognize that with the blessings comes responsibility.

Read Luke 12:42-48:

In this parable Jesus used the example of an unfaithful servant who did not make proper use of what his master had entrusted him with. In those days unfaithful servants were commonly beaten by the master–that part of the illustration obviously doesn't apply to our culture. However Jesus' main teaching point does apply, "From everyone who has been given much, much will be demanded; and from the one who has been entrusted with much, much more will be asked."

Think about the Christians you met and worked with in the place your team ministered in. Think about their church facilities, the availability of Bibles and other material resources they have for ministry. Consider their standard of living, the homes they live in, the availability of adequate food and access to good healthcare.

Now list some of the resources you, your family and your church seem to have in abundance compared to the local Christians you ministered with on your mission trip.

_____

_____

_____

_____

_____

_____

_____

In the spirit of Luke 12:48, do you think the Lord expects us to use some of our abundance to assist our brothers and sisters in other places with their Kingdom-building work? In what ways?

_____

_____

_____

_____

_____

_____

Do you think it's possible for you, your family, and your church to make do with a little less, in order to share some of the Lord's resources with Christians in other places who have so little by comparison? List some ways you could do that:

_____

_____

_____

_____

_____

_____

_____

There can be no question that those of us living in the developed world have been blessed with an abundance of material resources. While we are free to enjoy those blessings–without feeling guilty, we must also recognize that with the blessings comes responsibility. I have to believe our Heavenly Father wants us, His children who have so much, to share with our brothers and sisters who have so much less.

Sources:

1. Global Purchasing Power Parities and Real Expenditures. The World Bank. 2005 International Comparison Program. August 2008.

2. World Development Indicators 2007. The World Bank. March 2007.

3. State of Food Insecurity in the World 2006. Food and Agriculture Organization of the Unite Nations. 2006.

4. Black, Robert, Saul, and Jennifer Bryce. "Where and Why Are 10 Million Children Dying Every Year?" The Lancet 361:2226-2234.2003.

5. New Life International Water Purification Systems. September 2008.

6. World Bank Website. September 2008

Day Ten Journaling

Spend some quiet time with the Lord. Thank Him for the way He has blessed and provided for you and your family. Then ask Him to break your heart with compassion for those who suffer in great need. Ask Him to show you ways that you can help in the Name of Jesus. When you're done, record your thoughts.

_____

_____

_____

_____

_____

_____

_____

_____

_____

_____

_____

_____

_____

_____

_____

_____

DAY ELEVEN

Don't Forget Them

American missionaries to Peru, Bud and Laura Lenz
and the children of their orphanage "El Arca"

For many people one of the highlights of a short-term mission is the new friendships made with missionaries and with Christians from the host culture.

The dedication, commitment, perseverance, and willingness to sacrifice displayed by missionaries are inspiring. Likewise, the simple faith and genuine joy often observed in Christians living in impoverished and sometimes oppressive cultures can be humbling.

But did you know that you were probably a big blessing to them as well? Missionaries often feel lonely and forgotten. A short-term mission team traveling thousands of miles, at great personal expense, to support and encourage the missionary in his or her ministry can be a great source of encouragement – a spiritual shot in the arm!

Indigenous pastors and their church members are also touched and encouraged when Christians from other countries are willing to travel far, and make great sacrifices, in order to join them in their ministry.

Now that your mission trip is over please don't forget them! Your continued friendship and encouragement can be a great blessing.

Read Philippians 1:3-5:

How did Paul feel about those who had partnered with him in his ministry?

_____

_____

_____

_____

Who were the missionaries or Christians with whom you formed a new friendship?

_____

_____

_____

_____

What was it about them that touched your heart the most?

_____

_____

_____

How did they receive you? Did they seem to appreciate your ministry efforts on their behalf?

_____

_____

_____

Do you think they would enjoy, and be blessed by, continuing a friendship with you?

_____

_____

_____

Would you enjoy and be blessed by it?

What are some things you can do to continue, and nurture, your new friendship with them?

_____

_____

_____

What are some ways you can encourage and lift-up those new friends?

_____

_____

_____

Day Eleven Journaling

As you now sit quietly before the Lord, ask Him to bring to your mind the missionaries, pastors, churches and individual Christians you met on your mission who may be in need of special prayer. Write those prayer needs down here and come back to them often.

_____

_____

_____

_____

_____

_____

_____

_____

_____

_____

_____

_____

_____

_____

_____

_____

_____

_____

DAY TWELVE

Bringing Home a Servant's Heart

Serving others can take many forms.

Days one, five and eight of this devotional guide led you to think about some of the acts of service you were involved in on your short-term mission trip. Just to refresh your memory, jot down a few of them here:

_____

_____

_____

_____

_____

Does it seem as if your commitment to serve others in the Name of Jesus was greater than normal while you were on your mission trip?

_____

_____

Why do you think that was?

_____

_____

_____

_____

Days two, six, eight, ten, and eleven all led you to consider some ways in which your mission experience could have a positive impact on your service here at home. Briefly review your responses from those days and jot down a few of your observations from those times of devotion:

_____

_____

_____

Do you think your commitment to ministry, or perhaps even your ministry activities themselves, will be different as a result of your short-term mission trip? In what ways?

_____

_____

_____

_____

A word of caution: Sometimes we can get caught in the trap of thinking our ministry activities have to be great and spectacular in order to be significant. That's especially true after an intense time of successful ministry working with long-term missionaries (like on a short-term mission trip.) However that's not the way Jesus sees it.

Read Luke 21:1-4

To those observing this scene do you think this woman's gift seemed small and insignificant?

But Jesus viewed it differently, why?

_____

_____

_____

As you're considering what ministry activities the Lord would have you involved in, remember it's not the size or visibility of the activity that matters to the Lord, but rather the heart with which you do it.

Mother Theresa, the famous missionary who spent her life serving the poor and destitute in the slums of Calcutta once wrote:

"We can do no great things, only small things with great love." [1]

Sources:

1. BrainyQuotes.com

Day Twelve Journaling

If you adopted Mother Theresa's motto as a guiding principle for your own life and ministry activities, what would it look like as you lived it out on a daily basis? Spend some quite time with the Lord. When you're done, record your thoughts here:

_____

_____

_____

_____

_____

_____

_____

_____

_____

_____

_____

_____

_____

_____

_____

_____

_____

_____

DAY THIRTEEN

The Big Presentation

Mission Team reporting back to the sending church.

Most short-term mission teams, and individuals, are asked by their sending church to report back to the church, usually with a public presentation. Depending on your background and experience, the prospect of making a public presentation could excite you or scare the daylights out of you! Either way, reporting back to the church is an important part of the short-term mission process.

Read Acts 13:1-3.

What happened to Barnabas and Saul in this passage?

_____

_____

Now read Acts 14:24-28.

According to this passage what did Barnabas and Saul do when they returned to the church in Antioch?

_____

_____

_____

In chapter 13 the church in Antioch commissioned Barnabas and Saul as missionaries and sent them on a short-term mission. Upon returning, Barnabas and Saul assembled the church and made a public presentation to report the results of their mission.

Public presentations to report the results of mission trips are Biblical and important. Why do you suppose that is?

_____

_____

_____

As you've already learned, the process of sending short-term missionaries is a team effort. It involves senders, goers, and host-receivers. The people in each of those categories play an important role in the overall success of the mission. In the case of the public presentation, the goers are sharing the highlights of the trip with the senders. The senders played an important role in making it possible for the goers to go, so it's a joyful experience for them to now hear the results.

Having the opportunity to publicly report back to your church about what God did on your mission trip is an honor that can also be fun and rewarding. Here are a few tips that will help make your public presentation to the church an enjoyable and successful experience:

▶ Begin by praying that God will guide and anoint your preparation and presentation.

▶ Prepare well. Don't try to wing it. The Holy Spirit honors good preparation.

▶ Don't overdo it. A common mistake short-termers make in their public presentations is including way too much information. There's a lot of truth to the old maxim "less is more".

▶ When planning and making your presentation try using this structure:

• *Use a written outline and don't stray from it. This will help to keep you from rambling.*

• *Give a brief introduction that explains where you went, what the ministry objective was and who went with you.*

• *Briefly summarize what was accomplished.*

• *Tell a short story about something you experienced on the trip that touched you deeply.*

• *If possible, show a small number of well-chosen pictures that compliment the points in your presentation.*

• *If time allows, offer to answer any questions the audience may have.*

• *Be sure to give God the glory.*

• *Be sure to thank your audience and all those who helped make the mission trip possible.*

• *Don't exceed the amount of time you were allotted for your presentation.*

Reporting back to the sending church is an important part of the short-term mission process. It can and should be a time of rejoicing and celebration as the church welcomes their missionaries home and marvels at the things God has done.

Day Thirteen Journaling

Spend some quiet time with the Lord. If you haven't yet given your presentation then ask Him to give you a sense of peace and assurance about it. When you are done, record your thoughts. Once you have completed your presentation, come back to this day's devotion and record how it went.

_____

_____

_____

_____

_____

_____

_____

_____

_____

_____

_____

_____

_____

_____

_____

_____

_____

DAY FOURTEEN

Ok, Brought it Home...
Now What?

*Small group Bible study is essential if we want to
continue growing in our relationship with Jesus.*

Our journey together through this devotional guide is almost over, but your journey with the Lord will continue all the days of your life and then on into eternity. It is my prayer that this guide has helped you evaluate and process your short-term mission experience and that as a result, you have grown in your relationship with the Lord.

My goal was to help you think through what the Lord revealed and taught you on your mission trip. I also hoped to help you discover ways you can incorporate those lessons into the practice of your faith – thereby becoming a stronger, dynamic and more engaged follower of Christ. Do you think that has happened?

List some changes that are taking place in your life as a result of your short-term mission experience:

_____

_____

_____

Hopefully by now you've realized that even though your mission trip ended on the day you arrived home, there was still a lot left to learn from that experience. That was the purpose of this devotional guide.

Likewise, even though you have now completed the fourteen devotions in this guide, there is still a lot of learning and growing left to do. That's the purpose of the rest of your life.

Read Romans 12:1-2:

In verse 1 Paul calls us to offer ourselves as "living sacrifices" to God. What do you think he means by that?

_____

_____

_____

_____

_____

_____

Did you experience anything on your mission trip that will help you better live as a "living sacrifice" for the Lord? What was it?

_____

_____

_____

_____

_____

_____

_____

In verse 2 Paul commands us to stop conforming to the patterns of this world. Did you have some experiences on your mission trip that infused you with a desire to be less worldly in your ways? Write about that here:

_____

_____

_____

_____

_____

_____

_____

_____

Paul then continued his imperative command by telling us to be "transformed" by the renewing of our minds. What kinds of things can you do that will help lead to a renewed mind and a transformed character?

_____

_____

_____

_____

_____

_____

_____

_____

_____

_____

_____

On Day Two you read Philippians 1:4-6. You spent some time considering the great truth that through the special experiences of your mission trip God began a new work in you that He intends to carry on to completion.

Now on Day Fourteen you are considering a passage from Romans that, if you follow Paul's instructions, will enable God to continue carrying out that change in your life. Living according to Romans 12:1-2 will result in renewal, transformation and a stronger, more dynamic you.

A moment ago I asked you to consider what kinds of things you could do that would help lead to a renewed mind and a transformed character. As we come to the end of our time together let me offer a few tips that will help you to place yourself in a position before God every day whereby He can renew and transform you:

► Make time every day for prayer and reading the Bible. Nothing you do will have a more profound impact on your mind and character than to spend time every day talking to your Heavenly Father, and reading His letter to you.

- ▶ Be an active member of a local church fellowship. I don't mean simply attending worship services on a regular basis, but actually being involved in the life of the church family. That should include participation in a small group Bible study or accountability group.

- ▶ Be of service to others through ministry. Talk to your pastor or other church leaders. Ask them to help you discover the ministry God wants you involved in. Few things will help us grow more quickly in our relationship with Jesus than to take our eyes off ourselves and focus instead on serving others in His Name.

- ▶ Be actively engaged in helping to carry out the Great Commission. Evangelism is a team effort that takes many forms and utilizes many methods. The process of leading a person to faith in Christ is usually a chain of events that involves numerous people over a period of time. Learn the forms and methods that best fit your personality type. Discover ways you can be a link in the chain of events that leads others to a saving faith in our Lord Jesus Christ.

- ▶ Support missions – at home and abroad.

Day Fourteen Journaling

In the introduction to this guide I told you that mission trips change lives and that the mission often ends up having been more about what God wanted to do *in* you rather than *through* you. It is my prayer that you have found those statements to be true and that this devotional guide has helped you to become a more mature Christian. Please share your thoughts and comments with me at: jim@bringingithome.us.

Spend some quiet time with the Lord now and thank Him for your missions experience. Record your thoughts when you are done.

_____

_____

_____

_____

_____

_____

_____

_____

_____

_____

_____

_____

_____

_____

_____

_____

_____